W9-AVM-274

Pebble Plus · Pet Questions and Answers

CATS

Questions and Answers

by Christina Mia Gardeski

CAPSTONE PRESS
a capstone imprint

Pebble Plus is published by Capstone Press,
1710 Roe Crest Drive, North Mankato, Minnesota 56003
www.mycapstone.com

Library of Congress Cataloging-in-Publication Data
Names: Gardeski, Christina Mia, author.
Title: Cats : questions and answers / by Christina Mia Gardeski.
Description: North Mankato, Minnesota : Capstone Press, [2017] | Series: Pebble plus.
  Pet questions and answers | Audience: Ages 4–8. | Audience: K to grade 3. | Includes
  bibliographical references and index.
Identifiers: LCCN 2016006905| ISBN 9781515703563 (library binding) | ISBN 9781515703631
  (paperback) | ISBN 9781515703693 (ebook (pdf)
Subjects: LCSH: Cats—Miscellanea—Juvenile literature. | Children's questions and answers
Classification: LCC SF445.7 .G37 2017 | DDC 636.8002—dc23
LC record available at http://lccn.loc.gov/2016006905

Editorial Credits
Carrie Braulick Sheely and Alesha Halvorson, editors; Kayla Rossow, designer;
Pam Mitsakos, media researcher; Gene Bentdahl, production specialist

Photo Credits
Getty Images: Akimasa Harad, 21; Shutterstock: Benjamin Albiach Galan, 5, deftrender,
9, Ermolaev Alexander, 19, makar, 1, 22, maradon 333, 7, Maria Jeffs, cover, Nataliia
Dvukhimenna, 13, PearlNecklace, 15, turlakova, 17; Thinkstock, sduben, 11

Note to Parents and Teachers

The Pet Questions and Answers set supports national curriculum standards for science related
to life science. This book describes and illustrates cats. The images support early readers in
understanding the text. The repetition of words and phrases helps early readers learn new
words. This book also introduces early readers to subject-specific vocabulary words, which are
defined in the Glossary section. Early readers may need assistance to read some words and
to use the Table of Contents, Glossary, Read More, Internet Sites, Critical Thinking Using the
Common Core, and Index sections of the book.

Printed in China.
022016   007713

Table of Contents

Who Hides in the Dark?

My cat!

Cats feel in the dark with whiskers. Their eyes see well in low light. They play at dawn and dusk.

Why Do Cats Meow?

Kittens meow to tell their mother they need care. A fully grown cat meows to talk to people. It might want to eat or be pet. Fully grown cats do not meow at other cats.

How Long Do Cats Sleep?

Cats sleep most of the day. They can sleep more than 15 hours each day. This helps them save energy to play.

Why Do Cats Hiss and Purr?

Cats hiss when they are angry or scared. Cats often purr when they are happy. But they also may purr when they are sick or worried.

What Do Cats Eat?

Cats are meat eaters. They get meat from wet or dry cat food. Cats need fresh water every day.

Does My Cat Need a Bath?

Do you take a bath after dinner?

Cats do too. They lick themselves

clean with their tongues.

You do not need to bathe your cat.

What Are Hair Balls?

When a cat licks its fur, some hair sticks to its tongue. The cat swallows this fur. It makes a hair ball. The cat throws up the hair ball.

Can I Let My Cat Outside?

Keep your cat safe inside. Outside it can get hurt, sick, or lost. Some cats can be trained to walk on a leash.

How Do Cats Land on Their Feet?

Cats like to climb. When they jump down, their flexible bodies turn in the air. Their front paws go forward and land first.

Nice landing!

Glossary

dawn—the time of day when sunlight first begins to appear

dusk—the time when day changes into night and the sky begins to get darker

energy—the strength to do active things without getting tired

flexible—able to bend

hair ball—a ball of fur that lodges in a cat's stomach; hair balls are made of fur swallowed by a cat as it grooms itself

leash—a strap for holding and walking an animal

purr—the low, rolling sound of a cat

worried—uneasiness about something

whisker—one of the long hairs growing near the sides of a cat's nose used to feel

Read More

Ganeri, Anita. *Kitty's Guide to Caring for Your Cat.* Pets' Guides. Chicago: Heinemann, 2013.

Graubart, Norman D. *My Cat.* Pets Are Awesome! New York: PowerKids Press, 2014.

Hutmacher, Kimberly M. *I Want a Cat.* I Want a Pet. Mankato, Minn.: Capstone Press, 2012.

Internet Sites

FactHound offers a safe, fun way to find Internet sites related to this book. All of the sites on FactHound have been researched by our staff.

Here's all you do:

Visit *www.facthound.com*

Type in this code: 9781515703563

 Check out projects, games and lots more at **www.capstonekids.com**

Critical Thinking
Using the Common Core

1. How can you tell if a cat is angry or scared? (Integration of Knowledge and Ideas)

2. Why do cats get hair balls? (Key Ideas and Details)

Index